THE $150K+ CLUB

Discover the Career Strategies and

Mindset That Separate the Top 10%

OLIVIA GAMBER

Published by Game Changer Publishing

Paperback ISBN: 978-1-961189-84-3

Hardcover ISBN: 978-1-961189-85-0

Digital: ISBN: 978-1-961189-86-7

www.GameChangerPublishing.com

DEDICATION

To my husband Matthew, my son Mason, my parents Tony and Sonia, and my team at Career Evolved, who all supported me on this journey. Without them, I would not have been able to make the impact over the last decade through the work that went into this book.

Read This First

Just to say thanks for buying and reading my book, I have created a custom career coaching training video for you that is unique, depending on your profile. All you need to do is take the 5-minute quiz below, and you will get a custom training video that addresses your unique situation.

Click this link or use the QR Code below

The $150K+ Club

Discover the Career Strategies and Mindset

That Separate the Top 10%

Olivia Gamber

TABLE OF CONTENTS

INTRODUCTION

To enter the $150k+ club, where you are now competing with the top 10% of earners in the United States, you will need to start to play a new game that is different from what you have played up to this point.

What I'm going to share with you is the Career Evolved perspective to career advancement. This will help you to shift your thinking away from conventional job search tactics to a powerful framework that's going to allow you to stand out and gain complete control of your career trajectory. This means that you will stop treating yourself like a commodity using job boards, recruiters, and online applications and instead begin to shift your thinking and focus into building strategic relationships. You will really start to build your relationship capital. To enter that $150k+ club, you have to play a completely different game than 90% of the people out there. If you're not playing this game, you're definitely not going to win. Your outdated approach will not work in the top 10% because everyone who's there is already making or going above $150K; they are already qualified. However, it's not about the qualifications. It's about your ability to get attention and influence executives. You can no longer rely solely on your resume to do the heavy lifting for you to create opportunities at this level.

This book is for high-achieving business professionals—people with a proven track record of success; executives and consultants who want to really upgrade their career; and professionals who are already playing at a high level but want to change careers and reinvent themselves.

This book isn't just for those who have not yet broken into the $150k+ club, but also for those executives who are already in this club and want to get to the next level – whether that is $200k, $250k, $500k+ – going up to the C-level, where total compensation can be in 7 figures. Regardless, this is where there is more competition, and you must become more strategic about how you market yourself, so you can break into these opportunities and stand out from your competition.

If one of those groups resonates with you, you'll get a lot of value from this book. However, to get the most value, you must commit to reading it from beginning to end. By the time you are done with this book, what I can promise you is that you are going to become a new version of yourself, and you are going to become a product that cannot be ignored in any market.

You're going to be able to own and dominate your market, get more attention, access multiple opportunities, and be well-compensated for the same skills your competition is being paid for. I believe this will happen to you because you're going to really focus your strategy on differentiating yourself from the competition. You will see that you have your choice of opportunities now, not just the hope that you can get a job. You will have the confidence of knowing that you have full control of your career. I can tell you that there's really nothing like finally being in that place.

So, the most significant thing I want to promise you is that you're going to leave with that type of mentality and the ability to create opportunities for yourself, regardless of the market conditions.

Chapter One

TREAT YOURSELF LIKE A PREMIUM PRODUCT, NOT

A COMMODITY

Before we can get into the new Career Evolved framework for upgrading your career, we need to start where most people are currently. Most people who want to break into that $150K+ are still in an old mindset when it comes to their career, and they're using a system that is broken. They're using a system that treats them like a commodity. What I mean by that is they are currently using job boards and different online platforms to apply for opportunities; it could be LinkedIn, Indeed.com, Career Builder, etc. According to Forbes, the problem with that is that only 2% of all applicants are even called for an interview. The rest go into a black hole. When we're talking about $150K+, everybody is qualified on paper at that level. With that said, you must rely on more than just your resume to do the heavy lifting to get opportunities. Cold applications are not going to get any attention at this level. Additionally, the $150K+ opportunities are rarely posted or are filled before they're posted.

If you're still going to keep playing the career slot machine of online job boards, slamming resumes out there, and submitting mass applications, you're wasting so much time because that is just not how the hiring decisions are made and how the opportunities are really created at that $150K+ level. I am the CEO of Career Evolved. We've now helped thousands of clients break into those $150,000, $200,000, $250,000, $300,000, and even several clients who have gotten seven-figure total compensation offers. So, we've seen it all at this point. And what we have found is that most of these roles, especially at the C-level and VP level, are never hired cold from a cold application. Instead, it's the connections and advocates within the hiring companies that make the difference. You are never going to be taken seriously at those higher levels because there's too much risk for them to hire someone cold off the street. The old tactics simply do not work if you want to break into the top 10%. It's a completely different game. You must be willing to do what 90% of the competition is not willing to do.

The cost of success rises at each level, and this is no different at the $150K+ club. So ultimately, you need to stop thinking that you will rely on a recruiter or a job application and instead begin to position yourself as a premium product by building connections with executives in those target companies. One of the most powerful shifts in thinking is when you stop looking at yourself as a commodity, stop thinking about resumes and job postings, and stop trying to fit

yourself into a box. Instead, really start to think about your strategy

and how you can get more attention and exposure to those executive

decision-makers. That's when you know you're not thinking like the

rest of your competition and are ready to dominate your market. You

have a solid game plan to stand out and get more exposure.

Chapter Two

THE IDENTITY OF THE TOP 10%

We have found that you need to have a certain mindset and identity through helping thousands of executives break through and really stand out in that top 10% earnings of the $150K+ category. Conventional career coaching and consulting focuses on your skills, interests, personality, qualifications, marketing materials, and tactics like a resume and LinkedIn profile. At Career Evolved, we focus on the root cause of what is blocking people from commanding the top

10%, the $150K+ income, which has thus far been elusive to them.

We employ a process called Identity Transformation. Using this methodology, we get down to the root cause of what's blocking people from getting where they want to be. As we move through that process and get to the root, we can usually see that the individual's mindset does not match their ambition; they're still waiting for someone else to validate that they will be worth that much income. They're not owning their value yet. The problem with that is when you don't own your value, you won't be able to convince someone else to see it. You will struggle to close that deal and get that offer. Identity must always come first. And this is really where we transform your self-concept (Make sure to take our high achiever quiz to see your profile and receive custom coaching at https://www.careerevolved.com/quiz)

Your self-concept is how you see yourself, and how you see yourself is what you project out to others. If you don't see yourself as worth more than $150K, then you won't project that type of leader or executive, and people will not see you at that level. This is because you won't be communicating at that level. This is why if we don't transform your identity and your self-concept—how you see yourself—there's no way that you'll be able to show up like a premium product and command that top 10% income. As I said earlier, there's a lot more competition at this level, and everybody's qualified. Now it's more about how you're showing up, your ability to communicate and influence these executives and achieve results through other people. It's less about qualifications and your resume.

When we begin to focus on your identity, we look at the three components: your beliefs, your habits, and your values. You must get to a point where you believe that you are a bargain for them to hire you at $150,000, $200,000, $250,000, $500,000+, whatever that income level is for you. If you don't believe you are a bargain to hire at that rate, then you're not ready to command that value. And if you've never reached that level, you need to really start to take a step back and think about what types of business outcomes you could drive and create that would send a very clear message that you bring tremendous value and hiring you would be a no-brainer. Much of this has to do with you—your self-worth, your confidence, and your ability to really show up powerfully.

When you do not have these positive beliefs or that they are under the surface, you get stuck. Sometimes you are unaware of how this impacts your motivation and drive; what you're showing up as, and your energy and executive presence is how others perceive you. If you're not really owning that executive presence, and there are cracks in your confidence, then there's no way you're going to commit to showing up and doing what you need to do to command the value you want from the market. So, this is where at the beginning of the process, if you are not 100% convinced that you'll get at least $150K, then you're not going to get it. We can give you the best strategies and tactics, the proven frameworks, and the keys to the castle, but if you don't believe in your capabilities and value, you will just end up sabotaging yourself and going back to your old habits. You may revert back to thinking that you're just lucky to have a job or that now is not the right time.

Speaking of time, procrastination ends dreams faster than they can materialize. It can cause you to avoid examining your career and prioritizing your career goals. This problem of not showing up and not acting can be a symptom that there's a self-limiting belief under the surface. The problem with self-limiting beliefs is you don't even know they're there. Did you know that 95% of our limiting beliefs are unconscious? This causes so many people to not pursue their goals. Under the surface, they either don't feel like they're ready, or they don't feel worthy. They don't believe there's more than enough opportunity out there.

Self-limiting beliefs and lack of confidence can cause you to get in your own way. You become stuck in your own head, not trusting yourself to reach that next level. You're not sure you're ready, and you're not sure you could actually get what you want. When this happens, it is an indication that you're not committed to the goal. You don't believe you can command it and are ready to do the job. These are the biggest things that keep people stuck and keep them at a plateau in their careers. They become more complacent and begin to settle. Next, they rationalize their behavior and just drag it out. It is a vicious cycle.

So many of our clients come to us with a variety of mindset blocks that they don't even realize exist. They are anchored in place by their self-limiting beliefs. One of the most common issues we see that can cause this is related to people who are stuck in a toxic work environment. It may be that they have a boss who is toxic, doesn't validate them, is constantly asking for more, and expects them to work

24/7. There are no boundaries. When people have been in these types of environments for extended periods, they lose their confidence because their environment hasn't validated them. They've been behind the scenes and are not feeling seen and heard. Those folks have a really hard time believing anyone outside of that type of experience exists because they've been stuck in a toxic work environment for so long. This can cause them to internalize these self-limiting beliefs, and it really kills their motivation. They may abandon their dreams and commitment to work to get to the next level.

The areas we discussed above are what we examine when working with our clients. We shed light on the truth and then work to get to the root cause of what's really holding back the person from making things happen. We ask them questions like, "Why did you stop showing up for yourself every day?" Really starting to peel back the onion with that question and many other related questions is when you can start to see what's been really blocking the client.

Understanding the "why" causes a shift in the person's mindset to occur. That shift always starts with the inside of them because they are the product. They're the people that need to market themselves. No one can do it for them.

Everything begins with you, and really owning your identity is the key to your success. You must remove all the blocks and self-limiting beliefs that keep you stuck. To illustrate this, let me tell you about a client of ours. She was at her company for 20 years when we began working with her on her mindset, helping her really transform her identity. We were on a call a few weeks after beginning the mindset work, and she proudly proclaimed, "I quit my job, I burned the boats, I have really big goals. I've already got 30 conversations on the calendar for the next two weeks!" For her to just walk away from a company where she worked 20 years before getting another job is incredible. It shows that she now has a level of conviction and belief that nothing will stop her now. She is no longer in her own way with her self-limiting beliefs and the self-sabotaging behavior that kept her stuck for years.

We see another pattern again and again. People get stuck when they don't make time for their careers, and they continue to put everyone first. We see busy executives who are working 60-plus-hour work weeks, and they eventually get burned out. They're ready to move on, and they're ready to be empowered. They're ready to make a change. They're ready to get paid their value, but somehow, they end up stuck in the hamster wheel because they can't make space to prioritize themselves. That's a big block where constantly putting the organization above your own well-being is preventing you from achieving the goals you really want. There is a big shift that you need to make so you can really prioritize your future. If you're ready for bigger, you've got to make that commitment. You need new beliefs, new identities, new habits.

If your daily habits do not align with your vision and goals, it won't happen. Everything you're doing is just words. You will only achieve your goals if you show up every day to connect with the market. If you can't or are unwilling to do that, then the commitment level is not there. When we see those less committed clients, it always boils down to the problem -- a self-limiting belief that they haven't been able to identify or change and unpack so that they can stop getting in their own way. You must be consistent. You must show up every day and commit the time needed to confidently go from point A to point Z. You must create the habit of believing in yourself and seeing your value.

Something most people don't realize is that there's another level of commitment and discipline required at each level of income that you must master, and that commitment and discipline will become a part of who you are. Most of our clients are extremely committed. They have a seven-day-a-week ritual. They're hyper achievers. They're the top 10%, top 5%, C-level executives. What we learned about them is that they are extremely disciplined. They live and die by their calendar.

If you want to change your identity, look at where your time is going, how much of it is actually going toward your goals each day, and how much is going toward the other things you *must* do. Understanding the focus of your efforts is essential to knowing where your mindset needs to shift. You must remove the self-limiting beliefs so you can truly focus on what is important and then move forward. Our successful clients who are at or above the $150K level understand that it is 80% mindset and 20% strategy and tactics. Getting your mindset in order is the key. No strategy or tactic will work until you can upgrade your mentality and modify how you're showing up.

Our process has been tested on thousands of executives and has been proven effective. We know how to help our clients get these

$150K+ job offers. What we have found is there are two types of people when they first start this new strategy. The first group is like John. He was doing outreach daily. He was showing up. He was working on the process. He was calling a ton of executives, yet none of the opportunities were going anywhere. He swore he was placing the calls, saying the right things, and following the plan; however, he also said that there was zero momentum building. After we really shed light on what was going on, we discovered that he didn't have the right intention behind his actions. You cannot fake intention and energy. Executives are way too savvy; they will pick up on this. If you're just going through the motions and you're not really showing up in a way that's adding value, it's not going to work. It's all that identity that we talked about earlier. Being in the right mindset is going to be 80% of your success in breaking through to that top 10%, $150K+ level.

On the flip side, let's talk about Missy. She was a star client and a total rock star who knew her value and trusted herself to command that value. And she wasn't overcalculating her every move or every word. She had a strong presence. She took decisive action. She had strong convictions, and she showed up to do outreach, eager and excited to connect and really get her brand out there. She showed up detached from the outcome, actively listening in service to everyone she spoke to. Missy became a magnet for opportunities. After 30 days of executing our process, she had more offers than she knew what to do with.

The key shift here is really about how people were showing up. This is really more important than the tactics themselves. Because when you're showing up in service and leading with value, you're going to attract way more back to you than when you're showing up, letting everyone know you need a job. It's a completely different mindset because if you let everyone know you need a job, well, then great, that adds no value to anybody. If you lead with value and in service, you'll get way more back because people can now see how they can benefit from that value.

A lot of our executive clients come to me and say, "Olivia, what if I just give away too much? They take all my ideas, and I don't get paid for that."

My response is that's the wrong mindset to have. This is about having an abundance mindset, and quite frankly, if someone can solve a complex business problem in a one-hour phone call, it wasn't that big of a problem.

When demonstrating your value, have boundaries with them on how much you're going to do for them before you're hired. This is more about showing up and allowing them to experience your value and not needing to be attached to selling and convincing them. You know you're in the identity phase when you no longer need them because you're not looking for any one person's validation. You already own your value. That means you know the $150,000, $200,000, $250,000+ is coming for you. It's not a matter of if, but when. So, don't let any one company influence your belief and conviction level to that goal at that point. That's the mindset that is required to be able to get multiple $150K+ offers. It's just a really strong mindset, and this is where we see people get stuck. Most people don't have a strong mindset.

Quite frankly, most of the planet is living in a survival mindset, and they're not thinking about how to thrive and get to that top 10%. One of the biggest areas that influence your identity is your environment. If you're surrounded by a group of people that aren't thinking big and who aren't in that top 10%, it will be really hard for you to believe that you are ready for that top 10%. This is because you have no one to model after in your environment.

What is worse is that you have people who lack ambition and

don't want you to go after your goals. It's so important that you realize that what you have here will not get you there. There will be changes in how you're moving, who you're surrounding yourself with, where your attention is going, and with your habits. The best way to start claiming this new identity is to show up daily with new habits and then move as if that's who you are right now.

However, this is easier said than done. You've got to start to get clarity on who you want to be and how that person moves differently than the way you are moving right now. If you can't identify with that, nothing will change because identity always comes first. You can easily get another job, but to see a big breakthrough and get into $150K+ (if you've never done that before, just know it is going to be a completely new version of you), you're going to need to really up-level and be more personally accountable. You must do more personal development and self-work because you're not going to get there without an upgraded mindset that matches your ambition level.

24

Chapter Three

TOP 10% HABITS

Now you're aware that identity is the root cause of your problem with getting to that next level, the $150K+ club. You know that a new version of you needs to come out before this is going to happen. One of the best ways to begin reinventing yourself and upgrading your identity is through new habits. This is what primes the new identity and allows you to embody the new identity. It's the way that you're able to really train your mindset and show up more committed to this outcome.

We have found that there are key habits in that $150K+ club—the top 10%—which are a lot deeper than just how you start your morning. It's how you think, how you move; what you prioritize; what you value, and where your attention is going.

At my company, Career Evolved, we always say this to our clients and our team members. We believe that the universe rewards who you are, not what you want. And the best way to prime and embody a new identity is by integrating those new habits. So, we've gone ahead and captured *the top habits of the top 10% of earners.*

FINANCIAL GOALS

The first habit I'm going to start with has to do with financial goals. If you are focused on earning more income and increasing the value you're getting for your skills, then you need to set specific financial goals. According to our experience working with thousands of executives already earning above $150K, they have a very specific and clear target goal for their earnings, annual income, and financial success. They're also thinking about how they will build wealth, the back-end compensation, bonuses, and stock options. They know exactly what they want, and they have it clearly defined.

We have found that many of our clients who come to us don't know what they're worth, nor do they have a clear financial goal. They are not in the mindset of really planning ahead for their financial future. Instead, they're more focused on the overwhelm. They don't know what they want, and they don't know how they're going to get it. They're hoping they can get that $150K+, but they don't have a commitment or specific goal to achieve it.

This is a big first step—getting specific and clear goals because, without a clear vision, you have nothing to work toward. Having a vision attached to a financial goal is crucial if you are focused on breaking through and entering that $150K+ club and getting clear on that target.

CONTINUOUS LEARNING

The next habit is continuous learning. We found that the top 10% of professionals already earning $150K+ are focused on professional development. They are personal and professional development junkies. They go to conferences, read books, they listen to podcasts, and attend webinars. They're picking up skills, learning new software, and learning about the future of their markets. That is what the top 10% do—they're constantly evolving so they can stay relevant. Regardless of how the market is shifting, they continue to shift and evolve with it, and that requires continuous learning and commitment to growth, staying sharp, and being relevant.

STRONG WORK ETHIC

The next habit is related to the importance of having a strong work ethic. Most people on the planet do not have a high level of discipline. That is because having a high level of discipline is a high level of commitment to goals as well. Doing whatever it takes, even if it means going the extra mile to ensure they exceed expectations.

There are a lot of people out there who constantly say, "It's hard—things are hard out there!" These people just continue to repeat, "It's hard, it's hard, it's hard." There comes a point where you're either more committed to believing that everything is hard and blaming all the external factors, or you're committed to doing the work and taking the necessary steps to achieve the outcome you want. Our clients are truly driven; they are incredibly committed to their goals, and they persistently show up every day until they achieve their goals.

Their work ethic, discipline, and consistency make them elite professionals; they are willing to put in the time to not only do the uncomfortable daily, but become masters at what they do and continue to grow through it. Growth happens on the other side of your comfort zone. Anything that's worthwhile, any success, is going to come at a higher price tag. Our clients are willing and committed to paying that price, even if it means they have to do more reps to gain the skills and overcome their blind spots.

TIME MANAGEMENT

The next habit is time management. Now, this is tough, and we see this happening with clients who are unemployed and have to manage their own time. When they show up to their desk to work on their job search and get their career moving forward, the top 10% not only live and die by their calendar, but they're really protective of their time, and they make sure that their time is going toward their goals. They prioritize themselves and their goals, and that's where they put a lot of their attention so they can drive big results.

Being able to control where your attention is going, being disciplined enough to manage yourself (because no one else is going to be watching over your shoulder), honoring your time, and showing up to commit to the task attached to that time, this is a really big shift for a lot of people. Most people are living in a reactionary mindset where they're just running around with chaos and overwhelm, and they don't have a game plan. So, on the flip side, we've got executives who say, "I have no time to dedicate to myself."

That is where we really need a higher commitment level because you always have time—it's just not a priority. So being willing to make sacrifices on time and really make those adjustments is a big shift for our clients to be able to make this breakthrough for themselves.

NETWORKING & RELATIONSHIP BUILDING

The next habit is networking and relationship building. Most executives that are above the 10% level understand the importance of relationship building, and they understand that the best opportunities are connected to those executive relationships because those are the folks who can hire you. Building their trust and getting exposure to them is a key shift for people to move toward. If you're going through the old paradigm of relying on a resume and a job board, you're not focused on the things that are going to allow you to win at this level. It's all about building strategic relationships with executives and really starting to get more executives to know who you are and the value you bring. That is the best way to manage your career and make it a priority and a habit. Most people just focus on networking and relationship building when they need a job.

Then they're leading with the resume, it's a very reactionary conversation, and it kills the connection. When you can come in and really lead with value and learn how to truly build connections and strategic business relationships, you're going to be unstoppable at creating opportunity. You'll be able to really drive your career at the pace that you want to go rather than waiting for an organization to continue to promote you.

EMBRACE CHALLENGES AND RISKS

The next habit is embracing challenges and risks. The top 10% of earners understand that growth happens on the other side of their comfort zone. They're willing to take calculated risks because they understand that taking risks can lead to much higher rewards. This is something that a lot of people don't understand. You must be willing to make changes, try new markets, explore different companies that you normally wouldn't consider, and stay open-minded. Many executives that we talk to have very high-value transferable skills, and if they would just move from one market to the next, they would double their income. They could easily do that, but they don't consider it because it's too risky, and they've never done it, and there's a lot of fear. When you are trying to break through into the $150K+

level, you must be willing to take bigger leaps. This is really a big shift in where people need to get more comfortable with that fear of failure so that they can finally commit to taking that leap to make it to the next level.

MAINTAIN A POSITIVE MINDSET

The next habit is maintaining a positive mindset. The top 10% have an optimistic view of the world, and it starts with their beliefs about the job market. They know there's more than enough opportunity. You can now target the entire country when searching for remote executive-level opportunities. The sky's the limit, but you must have a positive attitude about the opportunity, about yourself, and about your ability to achieve your financial goals.

If you feel optimistic about yourself, the market, and your ability to achieve your financial goals, then you will be in a great mindset to overcome the adversity that may come along the way. Just face it, you *will* get punched in the face along the way

trying to go up a new hill and see a breakthrough. You're going

face resistance, but you must continue to have a committed and

positive mindset regardless of what happens. Keep moving through it.

That's where that positivity really serves you and why you're able to

stay highly motivated, regardless of what happens on any one day and

what the response from the market is. Keep showing up. It is

consistency and positivity that creates results.

VAL'S SUCCESS STORY

The last story is about our client, Val. By the time he came to

us, he was very discouraged. He was completely deflated from a year

of job searching and all the rejection. He was even stuttering when we

first spoke to him because he was truly broken and disconnected from

his values. He knew he was worth that $150K+, but his mindset was

so far from that, and where he was at the peak of his career because of the toll that the job search was taking on him. By using job boards and going to recruiters, he continued to hit a brick wall.

We started to rebuild Val's mindset by focusing on identifying all of the self-limiting beliefs that had built up over the past year of rejection from the job search. We have found that when someone is dealing with a traumatic work event like a layoff or long-term unemployment, it can take a toll on one's self-worth. To change his beliefs, we needed him to implement new positive mindset habits. This included daily gratitude practices and affirmations to help him own his value.

When one experiences a major setback in their career, like Val, we also need to help them to incorporate other habits to maintain a positive mental state, like exercise and getting outside. For Val, it came down to riding his bike every day so that he could release all the stress and anxiety from the job search. Slowly but surely, after a few weeks of daily mindset work, Val's entire tone, presence, and confidence in himself started to come back to life.

When Val started to genuinely feel positive about himself and his life, that also translated to more motivation for his career. Soon, he felt hope again and began believing he could still return on the same career trajectory. He was able to improve his self-esteem and self-image through these new habits. Essentially, he was able to create an entirely new identity by priming this new identity and habits daily through these new rituals he became dedicated to because of how they made him feel.

After a few months of doing the mindset work to build back up his beliefs and his habits and to get him into a more positive mindset, it was like a light bulb went off in his life, and his fire was reignited. Not only did he get a $30K plus increase, but he was able to improve his life with a new relationship and dramatically improve his mental and physical health.

Chapter Four

TOP 10% POSITIONING:

When we meet many high-achieving, ambitious professionals who've hit a rough career patch and plateaued in income, we have found that they are still positioning themselves as a commodity rather than a premium product. When I say positioning in marketing, it refers to how a company positions or presents a product to customers. It's about managing how the customer perceives you and then differentiating that perception from your competition.

Most high-achieving professionals are stuck in an outdated paradigm when it comes to marketing themselves to land a job they love. They are still using resumes, job boards, and a system that does not serve them. When you use a system that lumps you in with hundreds, if not thousands, of others all across the country, it becomes near impossible to stand out, especially at that $150K+ level. What's worse is using this system that lumps you in with a bunch of other resumes is positioning you as a commodity. Whether you like it or not, if you're starting your process there, just slamming out a bunch of job board applications, the message you're sending is, 'I need a job,' and that positioning is not going to get a lot of attention, especially at that higher level because everybody who is there is qualified. On paper, it's really tough to stand out when you continue to just use an old process that does not allow you to get more attention and make more people aware of your value. If you finally get a call from using that process, you're speaking to a gatekeeper and a recruiter, you're talking about your resume, and you're having the exact same conversation that everybody else has. So again, you continue to treat yourself like a commodity, and you get the same results as everybody else who feels lucky to get a job. They don't feel like they're in control of their career. That's how the majority, 90% of the folks out there, are operating.

To get to the $150K+, that top 10%, you need to be positioning yourself as a premium product. This process starts the moment you make contact with the company. You're either leading with the resume and a job board, or you're leading with strategic relationship building and connections. Remember, at this elevated level, everyone is qualified. The most significant ways to set yourself apart are through your presence, messaging, and communication of your unique value proposition.

Most of our clients, even our most elite clients who are CMOs, are amazing marketers. They're so great at marketing products and services. They're brilliant. But when it comes to marketing themselves, they have a lot of blind spots because they're too close to it to really detach and look at themselves objectively; to look at their skills and the business outcomes that they can drive. The problem we see is that most of our executive clients have so much experience— some with a decade of experience and some more than two decades. There's so much they could do, and they try to communicate all of it at once, then overwhelm their audience. That message also positions them as a commodity because they're saying when they show up open to everything, "I'll take anything." They come across as a jack of all trades and a master of none.

If you want to position yourself as a premium product, you have to move away from being seen as just a jack of all trades and really focus on the value you can bring to the business and what makes it a bargain to hire you at least at $150,000 to $250,000, $300,000 plus.

42

Tell them the ways that you could drive millions of dollars of impact for their company. What would they be spending if they were to outsource what you offer to consulting companies? What are the costs if they don't resolve the problems that you could solve for them? Until you start to think about business value, you won't get the attention of those VP and C-level decision-makers who can pay you at least $150K because they're thinking at more of a 30,000-foot view. If you're still talking about bullets on your resume or the job boards and what you saw in the job posting, you'll lose their attention quickly because often those job descriptions don't match reality and what's going to drive that hiring decision.

What will drive that hiring decision is that there's usually only one, two, or three big burning business problems that that leader is focused on that they know they need to resolve. They want to know that they can trust you to take that off their plate and that you understand that problem better than they do. But if you're busy talking about your resume and background, you won't resonate with that leader because all they care about is, "Can you solve my problem?" If you're not in that mindset of positioning yourself as a solution to big business problems, then you're just going to sound like everybody else who's talking about their resume, talking about their background, and it's complete white noise. You're positioning yourself as a commodity because you're having the same conversation as your competition. We already talked about that earlier. If you're relying on your resume and qualifications to get attention, you'll lose.

It's a different game when we're talking about the top $150K+ club. You need to uplevel your ability to position yourself as a premium product, as a solution to big business problems that make it obvious that hiring you at $150K+ or higher would be a bargain. So that is really about how you are coming in, and you want to make sure that you have a relevant value proposition because the key to getting attention from these executives is to be relevant. For the success of any marketing campaign, you need to have a very clear, concise, and compelling value proposition. And where most people struggle with this is they're trying to be too many things to too many people, and they're trying to be clever, and they're overcommunicating all that they can do. They're talking about their whole process. They're in the weeds, and they're rambling, and they immediately lose attention.

What we have found through helping thousands of executives create multiple opportunities in this market quickly and make it over $150K+ is that it comes down to getting a really tight message and that the C-level executive's attention span is getting smaller and smaller every year. So, if you want to influence the top-level decision-makers, you need to learn how to communicate in a more clear and concise way. This is a huge struggle for so many executives that we work with because they're used to over-communicating, over-explaining, and over-convincing because they want to make sure that the person hears all the value they have to offer. The problem with that is it's just too much to digest, and you're asking a very busy person to give you a lot of their attention and energy, and they're not going to be willing to do that until they know it's relevant.

Saying less is the way to capture more attention. This is one of the toughest decisions our clients have to make because they don't know what business problem they want to focus on. They don't know where they want to start. They don't know who they want to choose for their target audience. So, they get overwhelmed, and they get stuck for weeks, sometimes months, because they can't decide. This is why we have what we call the Market Validation Strategy (Go deeper on this strategy by taking our free quiz to get custom training for your situation at https://www.careerevolved.com/quiz). It is based on The Lean Startup methodology.

Let me explain. When you are a new product, and that is you,

you're a premium product that will be taken to market. You need to have a clear value proposition and a clear target audience. Once you have both of those, it's all downhill from there. The problem is we can't make that decision in a silo without actually connecting with that market. This is one of the biggest steps most people skip. They just start marketing themselves before they've really dialed their message in, and they wonder why it feels like their message is just hitting a brick wall. It's not resonating because it's not relevant. You didn't lead with the right positioning. When your value proposition aligns with the business leader's top priorities, they are more likely to agree to a conversation because there is tremendous value for them that is front of mind. When you position yourself as a commodity, you lead with the fact that you need a job, and that doesn't add any value to anyone.

In order to make sure your message is relevant before we take that message more broadly, we use our Market Validation Strategy to dial your message in to make sure it resonates with the target audience. This is done through having what we call Market Validation conversations to understand those business leaders' top priorities. Once you understand what their top priorities are, then it is much easier to make sure your message is focused on those business problems that are most important to them right now so that they have urgency and interest in hiring you sooner rather than later.

What slows most executives down from gaining fast traction with this process is they do not want to start having any conversations until their value proposition is perfect. The problem is you cannot create a relevant marketing message in a silo. You need to really deeply understand your target audience to make sure you are leading with the pain points that they want to solve. If you are positioning your value around a "nice to have" outcome and not a must-have solution to a problem, then you are going to have a lot more trouble creating interest and opportunities for yourself.

This is why we must get our clients to adopt more of the Lean Startup mindset where we are failing fast, failing forward, and rapidly testing and iterating the message and the target audience until we know we have everything dialed in and you are starting to see a pipeline of executive-level opportunities that you are genuinely excited about.

We found that if you want to position around a big business problem, then positioning around a nice-to-have outcome isn't going to create the urgency for that decision because it's just a nice-to-have. When you're positioning around a big business problem, you can create a lot of opportunities. We're finding that many executives have big business problems, but they don't even have time to create the job description to match their needs; they know they need help. They're all running a million miles an hour.

We've discovered that our executive clients get to a place where the roles are designed for them when they connect their clear value proposition with the organization's burning problem. They showed their value, they were less focused on job boards and resumes, and they stopped positioning themselves as a commodity. They no longer had the exact same conversations as their competition. They focused on owning their value, and they had conversations around the business value. They also recognized that there's no shortage of opportunity when you focus on positioning yourself as a solution to business problems.

It's such a big shift when you start to think of yourself as a premium product and then start to position yourself as a high value leader. When you start to have a clear value proposition that is focused on the business' top problems and the outcomes that you can provide to them, then you're leading with value. You're going to capture so much more attention because most people are leading with their resumes. Let me tell you, those C-level VPs don't want to read resumes. They want to know, "How can you help me? Can you solve my problems?" This is so much more effective than leading with a resume, and we find it over and over again when you lead with the resume—it feels like work for somebody to read it. They know you want a job, so there's no value there. If there's no job, they won't even have a conversation. Versus if you're focused on business problem value, now you've got their attention because you're relevant. This is a huge messaging shift a lot of our clients made. They were immediately getting so many opportunities with that big shift in how they were approaching their positioning. Most were not even aware they were positioning themselves as a commodity. Once they realized it, it was like a light bulb had gone off.

JAMES

I want to tell a quick story about James, who was one of our clients. When we met James, he had more than 15 years of experience doing a number of things: sales, leadership, running his own business, training, and coaching. Despite that, he was really struggling to market himself.

He was putting a lot of time into his outreach and networking efforts. He was having so many calls every week, but these conversations were leading nowhere. Even though his network seemed eager to help him, he still wasn't getting quality interviews from all the time he put into his job search. At this point, he felt like perhaps there just wasn't enough opportunity at his level, and he was worried he was going to have to take a pay cut to get back into the workforce.

The problem was that he was trying to market himself on two different paths at the same time, and he was getting nowhere with the conventional job search approach or networking efforts. This was because nobody really understood what he wanted to do and how to help him. James was facing a challenge that we see so many highly skilled professionals face—he was trying to be too many things at once. This seemed like a smart strategy to him because he wanted to keep his options open to create more opportunities for himself.

The reality was that his approach was causing the opposite to happen. By trying to over-communicate all the things he could do, he was diluting his message and leaving people confused about where he could add value. Once we got his value proposition focused on one area where he could add value to an organization and how he could really turn around an underperforming sales team and increase revenue, then suddenly, he had no problem getting phone calls with decision-makers who could hire him because his message was now clear and relevant. He had a calendar full of opportunities and conversations with the executives. So, having the right message is a game changer. It's all downhill from there. When you have the right message and the right target audience, you will inevitably be successful.

After just six weeks of doing outreach focused on his new value proposition, James secured two offers that paid him significantly more than his last role. When you learn how to position around the business value, you immediately change the perception of the value you bring to the table and are able to command more compensation for your skills compared to the average professional. This is because most people haven't taken the time to get strategic about their messaging and positioning to stand out from the competition as James did.

Your market validation does not need to be perfect because the market is always evolving. What you'll find relevant can vary depending on what's important in the industry at that time. It's important to be connected with your market and to dial in your message because if you're waiting until you have an interview to see if this is going to work, it's too late. There's no way you'll close that deal because you haven't taken the time to get to know your market and that audience like the back of your hand. You won't feel confident in your value, and they will easily see that through how you communicate.

Chapter Five

TOP 10% MARKETING STRATEGY

If you want to stand out and break into the top 10% and earn at least $150K+ a year, you need to be willing to own your personal brand and market that brand at a level that most will not commit to. Most professionals take a passive approach that is focused on recruiters, trying to convince these gatekeepers to create opportunities for them. They waste hundreds of hours applying to hundreds of jobs, only to be lucky to receive maybe one automated email back, if anything.

That's not only a losing strategy, but it's also near impossible to get a $150K+ opportunity through this process.

At Career Evolved, we call this "the career slot machine of death" because it takes all the power out of your hands and relies on a system that treats you like a commodity. What I mean by that is you're treated like a commodity because you're lumped into a pile of resumes that are entered into a database. It's nearly impossible to get attention because, as I've been saying throughout this book, everyone at that $150K+ level has the qualifications, education, led teams, and managed millions in budgets. You need to show how you are different and how you can provide value to the organization. That's what sets you apart from your competition.

Relying only on your resume no longer works at that $150K+ level. You must be willing to let go of that process if you are committed to achieving that $150K+ level. You must start to shift into, again, seeing yourself as a premium product that needs to be marketed with a strategy that is focused on getting the attention of those decision-makers, those executives who can actually pay you $150K+ a year. We have found a massive market opportunity at that $150K+ level, and these tend to be leadership opportunities. All the businesses across the country and worldwide are experiencing burning problems that need your leadership.

THE HIDDEN MARKET

Some people believe there's a hidden market with a database, a job board, or something secret you must find to tap into these best opportunities that nobody can access. But the truth is, the majority of these opportunities that pay $150,000, $200,000, $300,000, $500,000, or a million plus are attached to big, burning business problems. This is especially true when talking about the C-level. *You're not going to see those jobs advertised.* No big company wants to advertise that their CMO is underperforming and they need to replace them. Those are highly confidential searches.

There can also be new C-level opportunities—perhaps a chief product officer or a chief business officer. These are newer company positions that didn't exist before. You're not going to see those posted either because a lot of times, what's happening is there are conversations within the C-suite and the VP level for months. They are discussing their burning business problems. They want to know who can solve their problems. They discuss if they need to go external or if they need to hire a consultant. There are so many conversations happening. If you don't have a marketing strategy to target these opportunities at the business problem level, you're missing out and not tapping into 80% of the market. If you're still just focused on job postings, you've lost before you started because now, you're competing against the whole country. When you create a proactive marketing approach and focus on targeting business problems instead of jobs, you unlock an abundance of opportunities.

There is always an abundance of opportunity at that $150K+ level. The problem is you must be trained to see that opportunity, identify it, and create it. You need marketing skills to build that pipeline of opportunity for yourself. If you're not a marketer, you likely have not been doing this for yourself. When you're willing to shift into a proactive marketing strategy used by the top 10%, you can easily create a pipeline of opportunities that pay $150,000, $200,000, $300,000+ without relying on job boards and going through recruiters. When you do it this way, leveraging our Consistent Connection Strategy, there is little, if no, competition at all because what is happening is you're starting to have a conversation that none of your competition is having. They simply read a job description or go through that conventional job search process. This is where 90% of your competition is still playing because they have not made the shift that is critical to dominating at that top 10% level.

CONSISTENT CONNECTION STRATEGY

The proven strategy that we use at Career Evolved with our clients is called the Consistent Connection Strategy (Take the free quiz at https://www.careerevolved.com/quiz for deeper training on how to apply this strategy to your situation), which is essentially a marketing campaign to get more executives who can pay you at least $150K+ to know who you are and to understand the value you bring. Here is a really quick story of what this looks like.

RANDY

When we met Randy, she was a talented HR executive. She found herself, for the first time in a career transition, feeling extremely frustrated, deflated, and totally discouraged by the lack of results from applying online. All of her peers were telling her she was crazy to expect to get a VP offer at the target compensation she was focused on because they were saying that it was just tough out there.

Instead of listening to them, she shifted her thinking and stopped questioning if she would need to take a pay cut or settle. Instead, she started to see through our process that there was a full market of executive opportunities that she wasn't tapping into, and most of the roles she was tapping into through these high-level executive conversations were not posted. She was able to quickly build a pipeline of multiple offers, and she got everything that she wanted. She was able to select the best opportunity that aligned with all of her must-have criteria, and this was in a market where everyone was telling her she was lucky to even get another executive-level job. She ended up with a huge increase in pay because she was able to create demand for her skills by totally owning this process and getting her message in front of more of these executives who had burning problems that she could solve.

One of the key shifts you need to make, just like Randy made, to create a pipeline of these opportunities is to focus on generating brand awareness and interest. Here's the problem—Most people think generating brand awareness and interest simply means going out there, contacting everybody you know, letting them know you're looking, and sending them your resume. The problem with that is it goes nowhere. It leads with the message that you need a job that doesn't add value to anyone. Most of the time, when you have a conversation around you needing a job, people immediately shut down because they can't help you, and it goes nowhere.

Our shift with this process and why we know it's so effective is because we're not focused on coming out the gate selling, pitching, and convincing. The key to marketing is to create exposure and interest. So, going back to all the work that you've done at this point, you should have a clear value proposition and a clear target audience. At this stage in the game, it's all about getting more brand awareness and getting more executives to know who you are and the value you bring, then getting them to experience that value.

By leading with value and focusing on making connections, naturally, you're getting your value proposition in front of people and not coming out the gate with your hand held out asking for a job when nobody will be open to that conversation. So again, this is really about creating an experience of value from the gate. You will naturally create interest when that value is relevant, and your positioning is clear. Not to mention, you're getting way more exposure to decision-makers than we see with the conventional job search approach that has you wasting weeks trying to convince recruiters of your value who cannot even hire you.

We have found that you often waste your time focusing on recruiters because the recruiter is the last person to know about these executive opportunities. As mentioned earlier, these discussions have been going on internally for months. So, it's this stage that you really want to focus on with these executives, talking about their business problems and how you could potentially add value, insight, and clarity without any expectation that they're going to create a job for you. You simply show up demonstrating your value and know they want to solve these problems. And, of course, it's going to create opportunity.

This mindset is a big shift because it's so hard for our clients to let go of their old habits of just relying on job boards, recruiters, and resumes. It can be very intimidating for them to shift towards taking more ownership of their marketing to create those opportunities. Most people want to sit back and wait for it to come to them. We've learned that those executives, those top performers, are willing to build that pipeline and get their brand in front of the right people. Next, they focus on building those strategic relationships and expanding their network. This is what ends up getting them multiple offers. They aren't sitting around waiting to be called from one of the hundreds of applications they've sent out.

What we have found in this process (it's not just our opinion— this has been tested on thousands of executives, and this has been refined over and over again) is that outreach is the most effective and efficient way to get multiple $150K+ offers. It is going to give you more exposure to decision-makers than any other outdated resume or generic networking process because this is about the connection and leading with value. This is where we focus. The only thing that really matters in creating opportunity is having more conversations with decision-makers who can pay you at least $150K+. At the end of the day, this is all that matters. Everything else is a distraction. It's easy to get caught up in the LinkedIn profile or your resume having the perfect bullets and font. It's so easy to get caught up in where you can focus on your tangible brand assets when really, neither of those items—the resume nor the LinkedIn profile—is what really generates the opportunity. It's the connection. Yes, that matters, but they are really insignificant in the big picture of creating these $150K+

opportunities.

Note: if you take nothing else away from this chapter, it's important that you're willing to let go of outdated thinking and outdated processes and really go all in on mastering how to build more strategic relationships so that you can open more doors and opportunities for yourself.

Chapter Six

HOW THE TOP 10% SELL THEMSELVES

Most people who are attempting to sell themselves for opportunities that pay over $150K+ use the same framework, and they are having the same conversations. I say this because I've interviewed thousands of executives, and it all becomes white noise after a while because they are all going about that sales process the exact same way.

What that sounds like is they will come into an interview with a hiring leader, and they will use the standard question/answer interview format. It's a very boring conversation because they are having a conversation about their resume, about their background, about how many years they've done it, and it all sounds the same. They all talk about how they exceeded revenue goals. They're all exceeding quota. Everybody's managed teams. Everybody is sharing the same highlight reel, and it all ends up blurring together. It's nearly impossible to stand out because everybody plays with the same playbook. This is exactly why it's so painful for hiring officials to interview. It's difficult to tell who's going to drive results and who's just talking about it. When you can shift away from that conventional conversation where you're playing a passive role of just answering questions, you can actually have a bigger impact on that conversation and influence that leader by providing more value and clarity. You are able to stand out from your competition.

THE DOCTOR FRAMEWORK

The framework that we use at Career Evolved with our clients is called the Doctor Framework. This is all about you stepping into a more consultative sale. You can't come in selling advice before you have more insight and clarity on the current conditions.

Let me give you this analogy. If you're one of the best surgeons in the world, you're not going to immediately say, "You need surgery. Let me tell you how I could do surgery on you. Please do the surgery with me." Instead, you're going to ask questions. You're going to diagnose. You're going to run your tests; you're going to dig deeper and make sure that surgery is a fit. You're not there to push and convince because you know what you do and the value of it.

It's a big shift for our clients to really step into that doctor mindset where they are the expert, they are leading the conversation, and they're able to provide clarity and value because they are not used to taking leadership and ownership of that conversation. They're used to being more passive, sitting back, and letting that leader guide the conversation. This doesn't serve you or the leader.

Many times, when you're being hired for these high-level $150K+ roles, you are being brought in to solve big business problems. If you're simply answering questions without context, you could be speaking about stories that are not relevant to that leader. Instead of simply answering every question, our clients ask deeper questions to better understand the burning one, two, or three problems that are the highest priority for that leader and what they have done to try to address them. They want to get as much insight as they can into the current context and conditions. After that, they are able to position themselves as a solution. They become far way more relevant, and they keep that leader's attention.

The Doctor Framework is a big skill that our clients need to build because they're so used to just telling the same stories, and they don't know whether or not that would be relevant. The truth is that the leader doesn't really care about all your previous stories. They want to know if you understand their problems better than they do so they can be 100% confident you can solve their problems. So, unless you're speaking directly to their specific pain points and how you're going to drive results, you will easily lose their attention. You will lose influence with them because your message is not relevant.

The Doctor Framework requires a new mindset. Once you get really good at the process of consultative selling and you leverage this framework, you'll be able to stand out from your competition, and you will have a conversation that no one else is having. Everybody else will just be talking about their resume and their background.

When you shift away from treating yourself like a commodity and begin having customized, specific conversations that are speaking specifically to that leader and their problems, you will get and keep their attention. You will be able to influence them and get them excited because now you're speaking about the key outcomes that they're most emotionally driven by. You made the conversation about them.

People forget that hiring is an emotional decision. We would like to believe that it's simply made based on who's the most qualified candidate. But in reality, they are making the decision based on one, do they like you? And two, do they trust you? And three, do they believe you care about their problem as much as they do? If you're busy talking about your own background and your story, you are not resonating with that leader because, at the end of the day, that's not hitting on one of the three biggest emotional buckets that's going to drive that decision.

It is a huge shift when our clients begin to really focus on serving that leader. They are less concerned with pitching and convincing. Instead, they go deep, diagnosing and understanding. This is a huge shift because everybody's coming in with the "pitch and convince" approach to the conversation. When you show up with that mindset of needing to pitch and convince, you're creating more doubt because you're not speaking to what that person needs. You're speaking to convince them you're qualified to do the job.

What we really get our clients to see is that *you're already qualified, or you wouldn't be in front of this decision-maker. They wouldn't even be on the phone with you if they didn't see you as qualified.* The conversation needs to go deeper into them and their pain points. This is a skill a lot of people have a lot of trouble with because they are not sure it's appropriate to ask those questions. A lot goes into the mindset of allowing our clients to own this Doctor Framework, but once they do, they are shocked at the results—they're able to see the level of impact they can have.

JOVAUGHN

One example is one of our clients, Jovaughn. He was an operational executive, and he didn't have as much experience selling. He had so much value, so much education, and so much experience, but he was having trouble getting other executives to see and understand the value that he brought to the table. It wasn't until he stopped trying to be understood and stopped explaining all of his background, but instead shifted to focusing on understanding them, their problems, their pain, and their business that he was able to present himself with the most relevant experience and he kept their attention by allowing them to do most of the talking and showing up. He demonstrated his value through the questions he asked instead of needing to sell his background, which was not relevant to what they cared most about.

He was shocked when a 30-minute conversation turned into an hour-long conversation with an eager executive ready to discuss bringing him on board with the company. This is something that we have so many examples of because once you're able to shift out of that commodity mindset and really own and lead with all the value, you will stand out because nobody else is showing up this way.

Another great example was when we helped our client create an opportunity out of thin air with an executive that didn't even have a role posted. She showed up inquisitive, asking questions to understand their business problems and priorities, then she was able to share relevant stories and examples of how she solved those problems. This immediately led to a conversation about them needing to take her on for an executive-level opportunity.

We see it over and over again. The best opportunities happen when you are focused on getting those created for you. It is about using consultative selling to uncover the two to three biggest burning pain points that will lead to the decision. These pain points are not on the job description but instead are the emotional hot buttons that will drive that hiring decision. It's so important that you're able to uncover what those are and speak to those specifically to convert more of these conversations into offers. When you do this, you will dominate your market because you are positioning yourself as a premium product, and you are having conversations that no one else is having. You will absolutely stand out because of how focused you are on being relevant to them and how little you're focused on convincing and selling your background, which is exactly what your competition is doing.

This is one of the most powerful shifts we see that creates more pay, more opportunities, and more empowerment for our clients to really take control of their career trajectory and create more high-paying offers above that $150K+ level.

Chapter Seven

CREATE LEVERAGE TO NEGOTIATE

PAY LIKE THE TOP 10%

Owning your value allows you to command top pay because you are now focused on building a pipeline of multiple opportunities. At Career Evolved, we tell this to our clients every single day. We don't stop working on the process until you have multiple offers because that is ultimately how you create the most leverage—you are creating that demand. It's just like any simple business principle. It's the same with negotiations. There's only one you, and there are a lot of people that would want you, but they need to know about you, and you must create that demand.

The reason most people are struggling to create that demand is because, as we said earlier on, they're still using the conventional job search tactics that just do not work at that $150K+ level. The negotiation and your ability to command top value started way before this point in the book. That starts the moment you contact that company. How you contact that company influences how they perceive you and your value out of the gate. I cannot stress this enough: you will not have as much leverage for the negotiation if you haven't mastered the rest of the steps that came before this point. Our goal with anyone that we work with is to have multiple offers, which, as I said, is what creates leverage. You can then be more aggressive with your negotiation because of the demand you've created for yourself.

We have found that many of our clients have never negotiated in their careers. We've worked with thousands of executives, and it always shocks me when I hear how hesitant they are to negotiate because they don't want to rock the boat, they don't want to lose the deal, or they don't want to start the relationship off on a bad foot. It's important that before we get into the tactics, we first change your thinking about negotiation. You must realize that they are expecting you to negotiate.

They are expecting to see how you negotiate, and this is a great opportunity for you to demonstrate that because you will need to negotiate for the company. It is expected that you're going to be doing some negotiation. If you don't, you are definitely leaving thousands of dollars on the table. There are really three main levers that you can pull with the negotiation to create leverage for that top pay.

The first item is your current compensation. This is valuable leverage because, especially if you already got a job, it would be reasonable to expect you won't leave that job for a pay cut. You'll be looking for a pay increase. Most of our clients who go through our process of creating multiple offers are able to see at least a 30% to 40% increase in pay from their last role. Some of them see a 300% pay increase. It's all over the board. It's all about how much leverage you can create, how much you are willing to own your value and the results you can drive for that company. So, your current compensation is valuable leverage, assuming you are paid your value right now. If you're underpaid, then you definitely do not want to use that information because it will work against you. You do not want to disclose that when you're underpaid because they will be operating off that data point on where they want to offer you.

The second biggest lever that you can pull is the market value for your skills. It's very important that you get connected with the market and people in the roles operating at the level that you are focused on and find out the pay for those skills. This gives you valuable insight into what the market is currently paying. You can get this data from compensation surveys; you can do research. There are so many ways you can get this data, but it's important to remember there will always be a huge range. Where you fall is really coming down to that value proposition in your confidence, in your ability to create that value because ideally, you will be able to get paid on the top end of the market value because you are in this top 10% group that's really committed to building the skills and the strategy that we have here for you to create demand and command that value from the market.

The last piece here is the most important lever. It's the value of the outcomes you're driving. This is the most powerful lever to pull because, for many of our clients, they have skills and are solving problems that could make or save that company millions of dollars. When you're really confident in the results you can deliver, and you have a track record of success, and you know that you have a value that can create millions of dollars or save millions of dollars for that company, or you can accelerate their timeline, you are going to have a huge value proposition. If you're able to connect those dots and get those leaders to see that vision and really buy into that, then they will be willing to pay above market, especially if that's a really top priority for that business.

We see this all the time with our clients. They're shocked when they stop thinking that they have to get paid just that 20% more than their last pay and instead start to really get good at communicating their value at that 30,000-foot view and paint a vision that that leader can really see and feel. That's when they're willing to take that extra step. Consultants are paid significantly more for outcomes than many executives are. When you think the same way about your own positioning, and you stop thinking about job titles and job descriptions and instead think about big business problems and big outcomes, you will be in a powerful place to negotiate because that is what that leader cares most about.

KRISTEN

Here's a great example about one of our clients, Kristen, who was offered the VP of Marketing position. It was really exciting because she was breaking through to that VP level for the first time, and it had been a really big goal of hers forever. Because she was so excited to get that offer, she was really scared to rock the boat or negotiate. But of course, we challenged her to really own her value and to present a counter to their offer. She presented the counteroffer, which was a very bold response and a pretty big ask. The leader immediately, with a strong reaction, pulled back the offer and said he needed more time to think about it.

This is where it got really scary for Kristen because she did not want to lose the deal. But at the same time, she knew just how much of a massive impact she was going to make on the bottom line. She did not want to go in there knowing that she was going to drive all these results and feel resentful for what she was getting back for that. Once she got more connected to the big picture and all the value that she was able to bring to the table, she chose to stand her ground. He processed everything and came back with a better offer.

This can be a really emotional process. But once you understand your leverage and you stand strong in that value, you're able to really make some big breakthroughs in your ability to command that value and command top value for your skills. It comes down to how much leverage you can create and your confidence in the value you bring. I want to reiterate one powerful point here. The reason that our clients see huge breakthroughs in their income through this process has a lot to do with their mindset. It starts with that identity transformation at the beginning, but this is where we really get to see the identity in action because if you truly believe it's a bargain to hire you at $150K, $250K, $300+, then you do not allow any one organization to determine that value. You do. You don't give your power away because, at this point, you know you can build a pipeline and command that value from the market.

Don't rely on any one company to determine your career trajectory. You do this. This is one of the most powerful mindsets you get to be in when you go through this transformation, and you're finally there. We know you're here when you're willing to walk away from companies that cannot meet your standards. I want to leave you with one powerful thought to sit with when it comes to negotiation. You get whatever you're willing to accept.

Read that again. *You get what you are willing to accept.*

That means you must be willing to walk away from anything below the standards you've committed to yourself. We talked about this earlier in the identity habits of the top 10%. They are committed to specific financial goals, and they are all in with those goals. It's not a nice-to-have. It's a commitment level—it's a conviction level—it's a belief level. Again, negotiation is 80% mindset, and it all starts with your belief and your commitment level to that financial goal that you set for yourself.

Chapter Eight

MANAGE YOUR CAREER LIKE THE TOP 10%

Most people think that they only need to go through this process when they need a job. The truth is the top 10% are always thinking about managing their career by managing and maintaining those strategic relationships. You want to integrate this process into your habits and way of life, not just something you do when you need a job. Because there are so many opportunities, staying connected to the market has so much more value than just getting job opportunities.

You can get a mentor; you can get exposure to best practices. It makes you better at your job. It gets you connected to people who are achieving and doing inspiring work. It can be a source of motivation. It could be a source of expansion. It could be a source of growth opportunity. One conversation can completely change the trajectory of your career. You never know where those conversations are going to go. Professionals in the top 10% are constantly staying open and building and maintaining their connections.

The performers that are in the top 10%, who are not only going to stay there but also continue to grow, are going to surround themselves with people who challenge them, and those are the professionals you need to model yourself after. It's important to find someone who can see your blind spots and give you the insight you need because half the battle is being aware of your gaps. Many times, we don't have an accurate mirror around us to tell us, "Hey, you've got gaps here, here, here, and here." Our friends and family aren't going to tell us that because they're not where we want to be.

Be careful of getting career advice from people who aren't where you want to be because that advice is not qualified. Just like any premier athlete, the top CEOs, and the top executives, have a coach, and those are people who can help them see their blind spots and really start to take things to the next level. It's one thing to know what to do. It's another thing to actually be able to do it. Everything we spoke about in this book requires mastery. It requires repetition. It really requires being able to be an influential communicator and have emotional intelligence, marketing, and positioning skills.

It's so important that you realize that this is a process that you need to build on and sharpen your blade for the rest of your career. It's not just a one-and-done because your competition is constantly evolving and getting better at this. Invest money to make sure you are in the right rooms with the right people. As I said, one conversation can completely change the trajectory of your career and your life. The problem is most people don't look at themselves as worthy of an investment, and they are not constantly investing in themselves to increase their value.

The more you invest in yourself, the more the value goes up for you as a product. As with any serious product that wants to go to market and dominate its market, you will have to invest in advertising, coaching, resources, and training. This is important because getting access to top executives requires certain skills and connections. You must be willing to make those investments so you can access their time because that's really what it takes to get their attention. To build these habits and skills to become that premium product that can't be ignored in any market, you must be willing to do and take that ownership and make those steps and commitments to do what your competition is not willing to do.

If you're looking for more help and you want to go deeper, and you want me and my team to guide you through this process. If you want to make it happen faster, and you want to make it happen in months, not years, I encourage you to check out all the free resources that my company has to offer through Career Evolved. We can guide you to the social media platforms where we're constantly providing free training.

We have a custom quiz where you can get your high achiever profile. We can also design specific custom coaching for you, so you know the next steps on how you can really make the most of this strategy. You can go deeper by watching some training. If you want, we can get on a call, and we can have a consultation with you and see if it makes sense for us to work together.

I want to congratulate you for getting this far. Most people don't even finish a book from cover to cover, so you're already on your way to entering that top 10% and dominating your career. We encourage you to go step by step and implement what you have learned, then read this book again because the first time is just for digesting. The second time is really thinking about how you are going to integrate and implement this into your life and into your career because information does not lead to transformation.

At Career Evolved, we're not big on a bunch of complex frameworks and information. We're about implementation and execution because, ultimately, that is what leads to mastery. That is what leads to certainty, and that's what gives you that security that no matter what the market conditions are, you can create an opportunity for yourself because you've taken the time and you've made the moves to really master each step in this process. You will completely change your life and feel so much more empowered, and you will know that at any point in time, you now have the ability to create that opportunity for yourself and really be in control of the growth

trajectory for your career.

THANK YOU FOR READING MY BOOK

CLAIM YOUR FREE BREAKTHROUGH CALL

Just to say thanks for buying and reading my book, I would like to offer you a free 1-hour Breakthrough Call with my team where we can provide clarity on your next career move, and if we are a fit to help you, we can tell you exactly how. If not, you will still leave with value and clarity on your next move.

Click the Link or use QR Code below

Let's Connect on Social Media

Instagram: https://www.instagram.com/careerevolved/

Facebook: https://www.facebook.com/careerevolved/

LinkedIn: https://www.linkedin.com/in/oliviagamber/

I appreciate your interest in my book, and value your feedback as it helps me improve future versions. I would appreciate it if you could leave your invaluable review on Amazon.com with your feedback. Thank you!

Made in the USA
Las Vegas, NV
06 February 2024

85418419R00059